There are things I feel but never say enough.
This book is my way of telling you all the reasons you matter –
not because of what you do, but simply because you are you.

Life moves so quickly that sometimes we forget to say the words that live quietly in our hearts.

Maybe you never realized just how much light you bring, how deeply you're seen, or how much you're loved. I hope these pages help you feel it.

All the Ways You Matter: Things I Want You to Know but Never Say Aloud
© *2025* Hugh L. Macy
All rights reserved. No part of this book may be reproduced, stored in a retrieval system, or transmitted in any form or by any means – electronic, mechanical, photocopying, recording, or otherwise – without the prior written permission of the publisher, except for brief quotations used in reviews or critical articles.

Printed in the United States of America
ISBN: *978-83-978057-0-5*
First Edition – *2025*
Cover and interior design by Hugh L. Macy

You matter

because your story makes the world softer

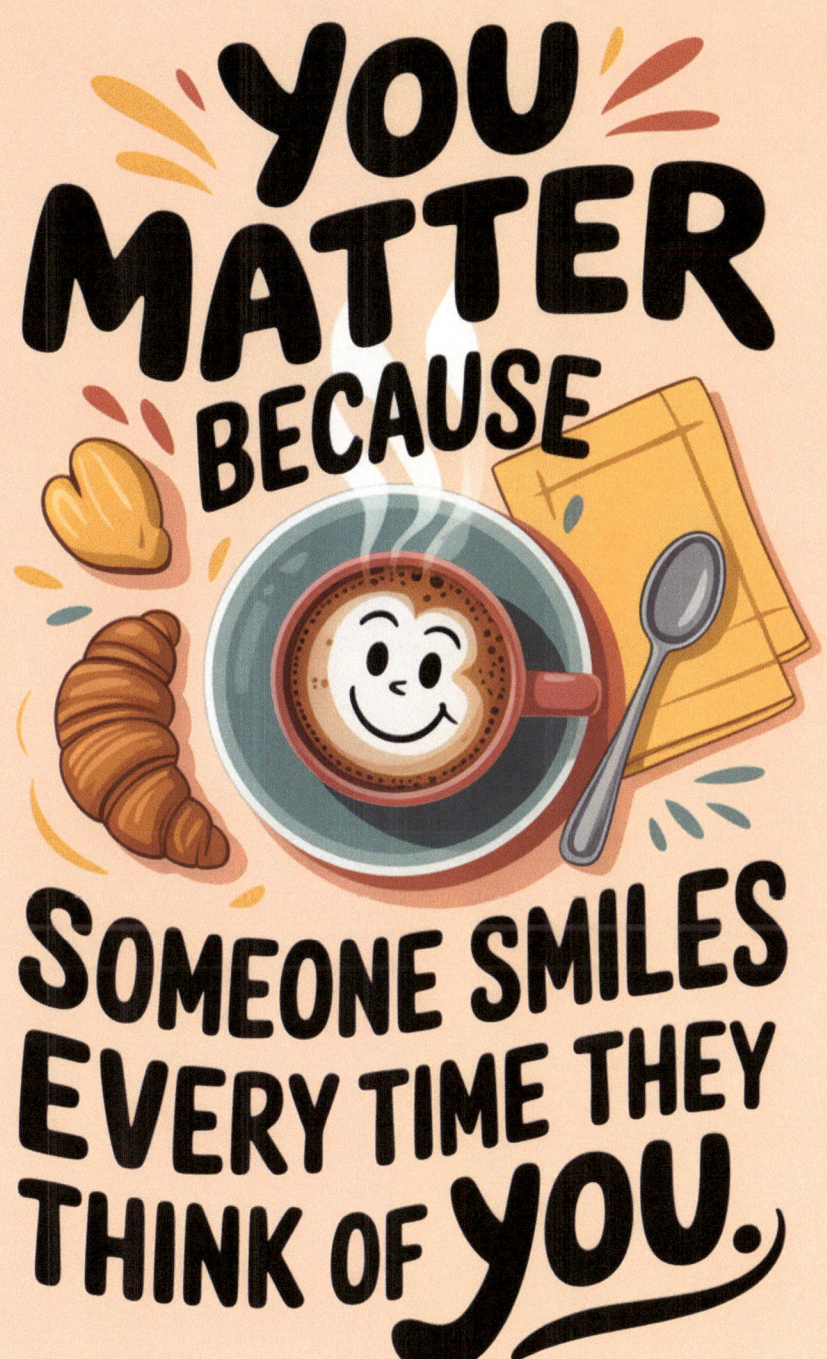

You matter
because you bring warmth, even when you don't mean to.

You matter

BECAUSE YOU NOTICE THE LITTLE THINGS NO ONE ELSE DOES.

You matter because you still believe in **GOOD THINGS.**

YOU MATTER BACAUSE

you're quietly doing good things when no one's looking.

 tap for say thanks

You matter because your mix of calm and chaos is oddly reassuring.

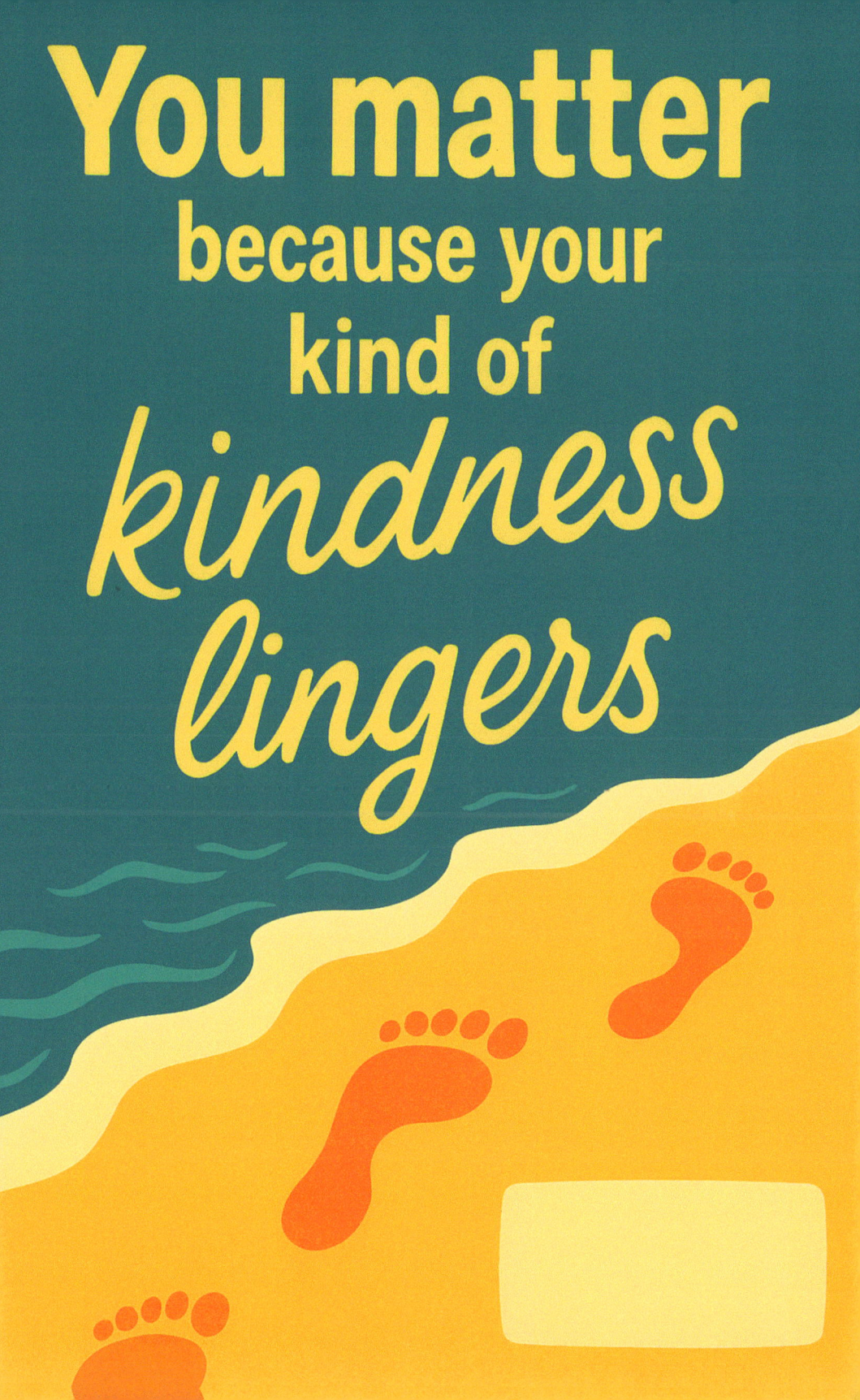

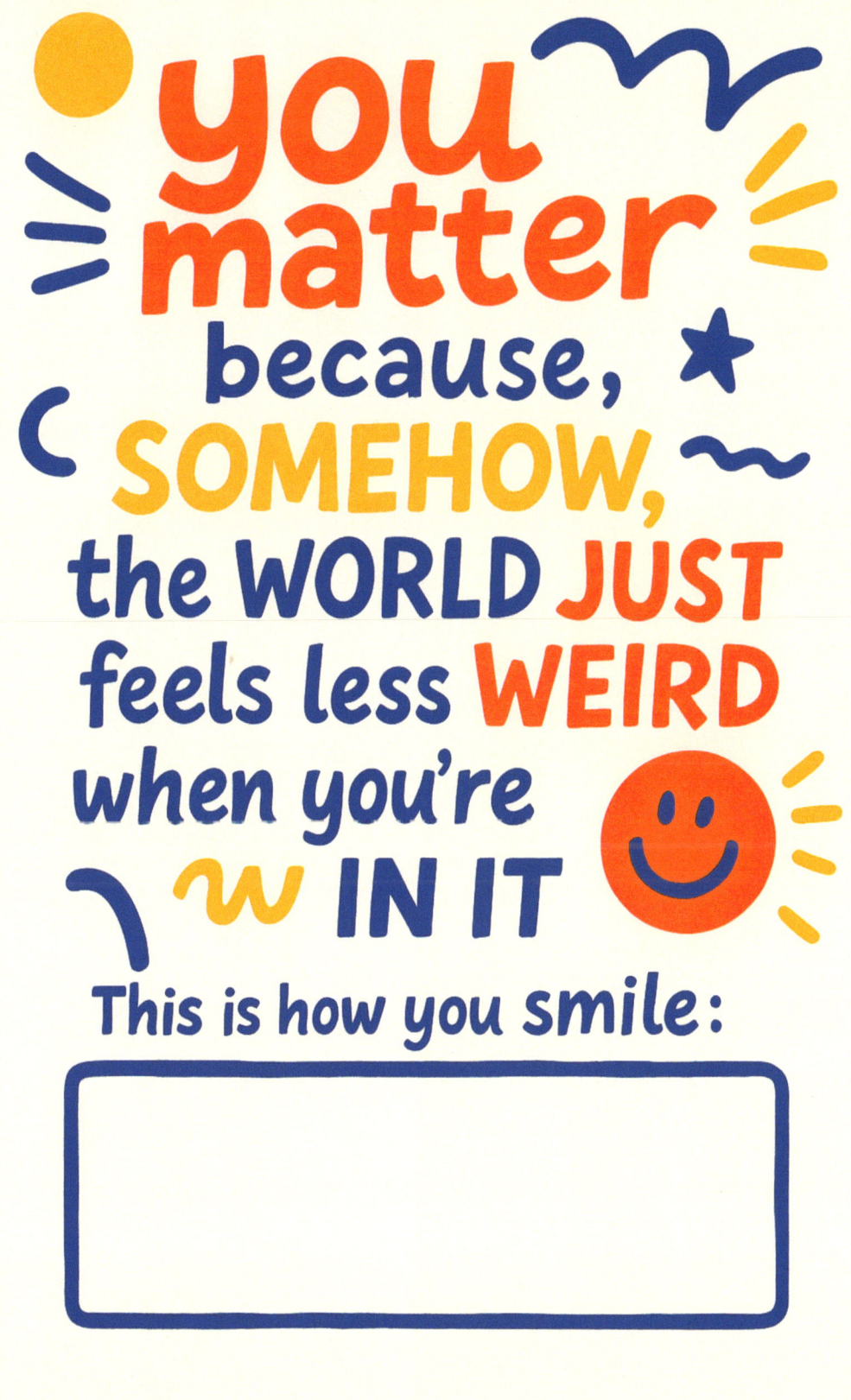

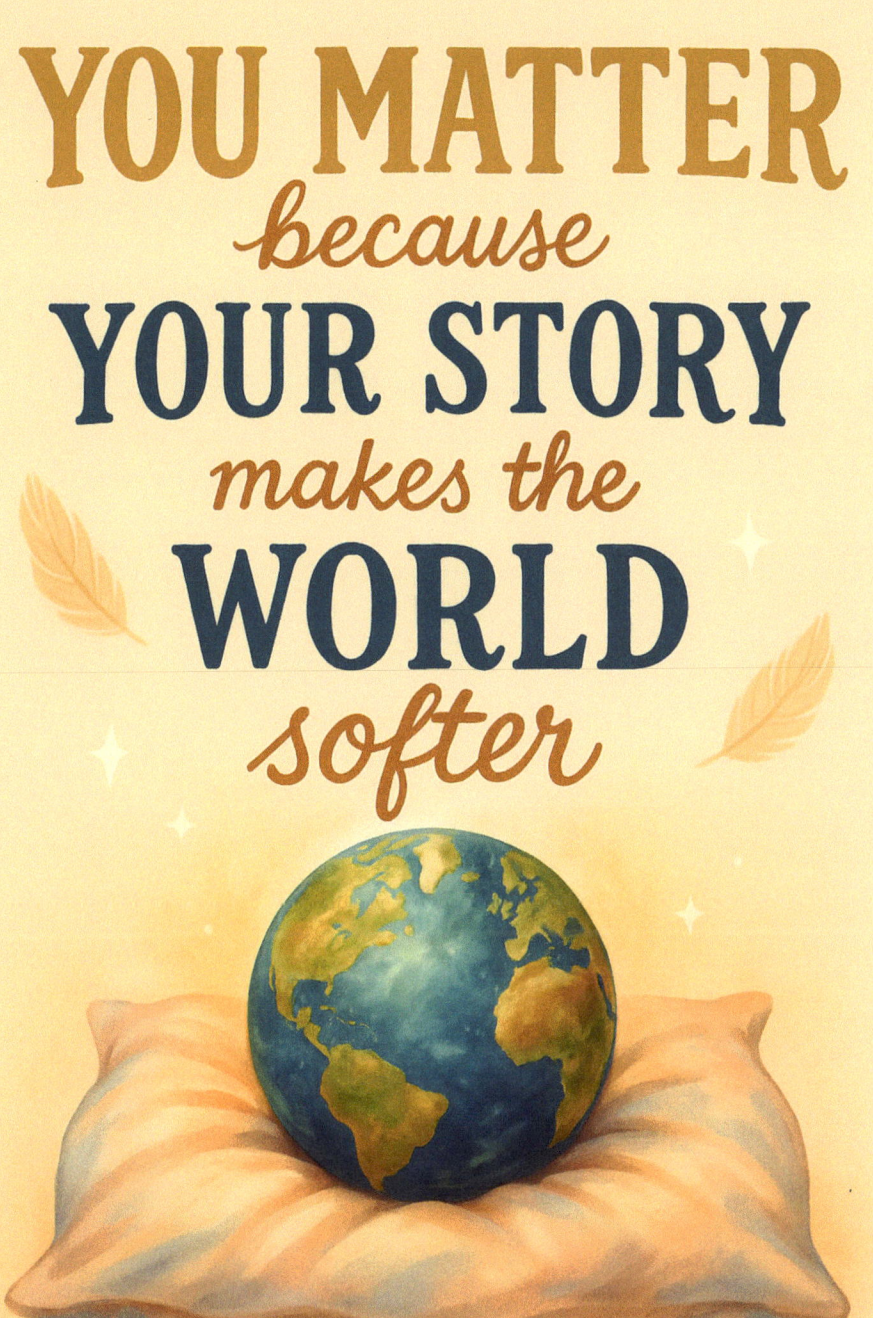

You matter because you try — and that already makes you rare.

YOU matter

because you **MAKE**

ordinary **DAYS**

FEEL like sunshine

YOU REMIND OTHERS WHAT REAL FEELS LIKE.

You matter.

because you are ...

You matter to me because...